DO YOU LIKE GE...

You might know that some germs

make fruit go rotten...

... give you food poisoning...

... cause diseases...

... and even make your feet smelly!!

BUT... is this all they do?
Do any of them do any good?

Read on...   **AND FIND OUT MORE.**

WHAT A LOT OF ROT!

In autumn, take a look at the fallen leaves or fruit in your garden. They'll probably be going mouldy. You might see some mushrooms or toadstools. Moulds, mushrooms and toadstools are called fungi. Some fungi are poisonous – so don't touch them!
Fungi may be big growths, like mushrooms. Moulds are much smaller. You can only see moulds when they clump together.

See how many types of fungi **you** can find!

HOW TO MAKE A MOULD FARM...

You can grow your own mould farm in a jar!..

1. Get some small pieces of cheese, apple and bread.

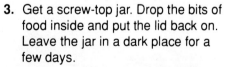

2. Dampen them and put them in a warm place for a few hours.

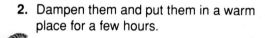

3. Get a screw-top jar. Drop the bits of food inside and put the lid back on. Leave the jar in a dark place for a few days.

Here's a good place!

4. See how many different sorts of mould grow in your mould farm!

Wow!

Lovely and rotten!

LITTLE ROTTERS

Your rot garden forms because there are billions of tiny mould seeds, called spores, floating in the air. When a spore lands on a bit of food, it starts to grow. When it's grown big enough, it produces more spores. These spores float away to set up home somewhere else.

Spores

A fruit-rotting fungus magnified 260 times

Our eyes aren't powerful enough to see objects this tiny. Scientists use MICROSCOPES to study small living things. Living creatures which can only be seen with a microscope are called MICROBES.

An ordinary microscope may magnify an object to many thousands of times its real size.

An electron microscope is even more powerful!

Perhaps your school has a microscope. If so, get your teacher to show you how to use it. Looking down a microscope is a bit like looking at people on Earth from a telescope on the Moon!..

What are you studying now?

Some kids looking at a jar of mould!

Let's take a look at the microbes...

All living creatures are made up of

TINY CELLS.

Your body is a huge pile of trillions of cells which live together.

Microbes are tiny cells too, but many of them live on their own. There could be several million different types of microbes in the world. But there are only five main groups...

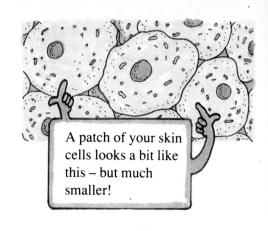

A patch of your skin cells looks a bit like this – but much smaller!

1. PROTOZOA

These are tiny animals. They usually live in water and can swim about to feed on other microbes. You can sometimes see them in pond-water. Big protozoa are about the size of this comma (,).

Amoeba

Vorticella

Paramecium

Yeast

Penicillium

Rhizopus

2. FUNGI

These often live as tiny single cells on either living or dead animals and plants. Sometimes they get together in a large group or colony which you can see. A mushroom is part of a colony of fungi cells piled on top of each other.

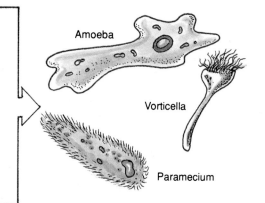

3. ALGAE

These are tiny plants which get most of their energy from sunlight. Many types live as single cells. Other types join end to end in long green strands. You often see these in ponds. Other types live together with fungi, forming growths called lichens.

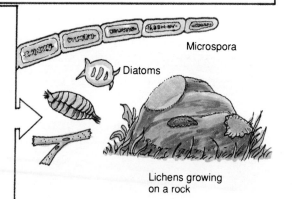

Microspora

Diatoms

Lichens growing on a rock

4. BACTERIA

These are a bit like plants and a bit like animals. Many of them can move about. They can make use of a huge variety of different sorts of food.

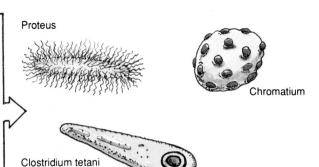

Proteus

Chromatium

Clostridium tetani

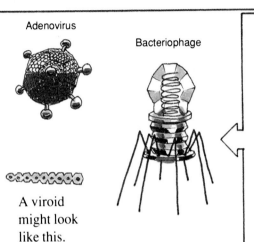

Adenovirus

Bacteriophage

A viroid might look like this.

5. VIRUSES

Viruses aren't cells – so many scientists don't think they're really alive! They're made up of bunches of chemicals which can get into living cells. Once inside, they hijack the cell's chemicals and force them to make more viruses. Bacteriophages are viruses which attack bacteria. Viroids have only recently been discovered. They probably cause diseases such as Scrapie and Mad Cow Disease. Viroids are so small nobody's ever seen them!

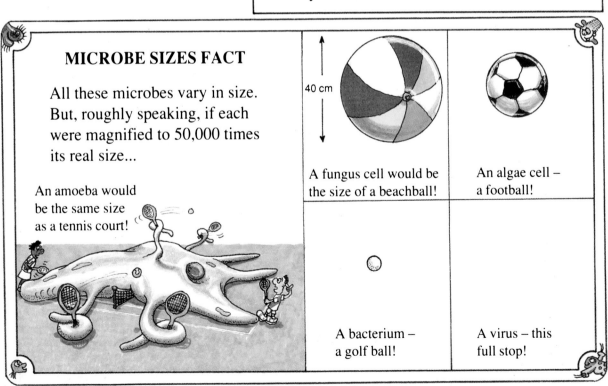

MICROBE SIZES FACT

All these microbes vary in size. But, roughly speaking, if each were magnified to 50,000 times its real size...

An amoeba would be the same size as a tennis court!

40 cm

A fungus cell would be the size of a beachball!

An algae cell – a football!

A bacterium – a golf ball!

A virus – this full stop!

WHERE DO MICROBES LIVE?

Almost any nook or cranny on board Spaceship Earth can be a home for microbes. Bacteria are particularly good at living in unlikely places. They can live and grow in places where most other creatures quickly die. Let's take a microbe tour...

Who's that?

It's Professor Noah Lott!

PROFESSOR NOAH LOTT ~ON TOUR~

He's an explorer!

ALL OVER THE WORLD!..

DOWN CAVES...

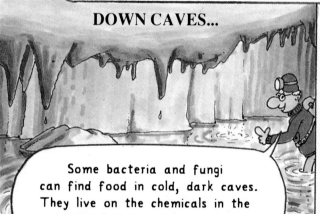

Some bacteria and fungi can find food in cold, dark caves. They live on the chemicals in the water. Some even live inside damp rocks!

ON THE SEA-BED...

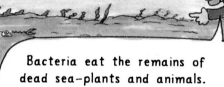

Bacteria eat the remains of dead sea-plants and animals. They form part of a deep, muddy ooze on the sea-bed.

IN ICE...

Some types of algae live under the sea-ice at the North Pole and in Antarctica.

IN SWAMPS...

Protozoa and bacteria live in swamp mud. They produce smelly gases which bubble up when the mud is disturbed.

Where else do you think microbes live?
Are there any living ON YOU??

YES! Billions of microbes live

ON YOUR SKIN!

There may be a hundred thousand bacteria on each square centimetre of your skin! But there's no need to worry. If you're healthy, most types of skin bacteria don't do you any harm at all.

The main places where bacteria live in a healthy person.

No matter how often you wash, you'll never get rid of all of them. In fact, doctors say that scrubbing too much damages the skin's surface. And that may help more dangerous bacteria!..

That's because your normal skin bacteria have learned to get along with each other and your skin. They don't damage your skin – they protect it! When you wash too much or use strong deodorants, you kill off the friendly bacteria. Then the dangerous ones can attack you!

The other main place where your
bacteria live is in your

INTESTINES!

If you're healthy, you may have about
five billion microbes living in your
intestines! Again, most of them don't
do any harm. Many of them do you
good. For example, one sort of bacteria
produces a chemical called vitamin K.
This vitamin helps your blood to clot
when you cut yourself.

Your intestines are a great place for
bacteria to live. It's warm, wet and
full of food!

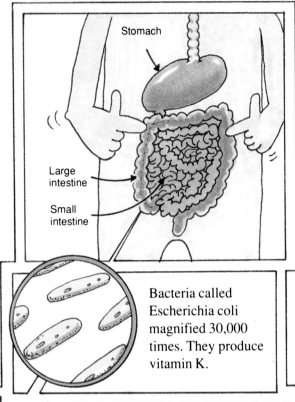

Stomach

Large
intestine

Small
intestine

Bacteria called
Escherichia coli
magnified 30,000
times. They produce
vitamin K.

Harmful bacteria sometimes
arrive with the food you eat. If
there are a lot of them, you
may get food poisoning...

MIXED-UP MICROBES

We usually live peacefully with our pet body microbes. Staphylococci bacteria live up your nose without doing any harm. Streptococci live harmlessly near your bottom.

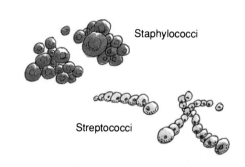

Staphylococci

Streptococci

BUT... if streptococci get into your mouth you may get a sore throat. And swallowing staphylococci can upset your tummy. Letting your microbes out of their usual habitats gives them a holiday – they run wild!..

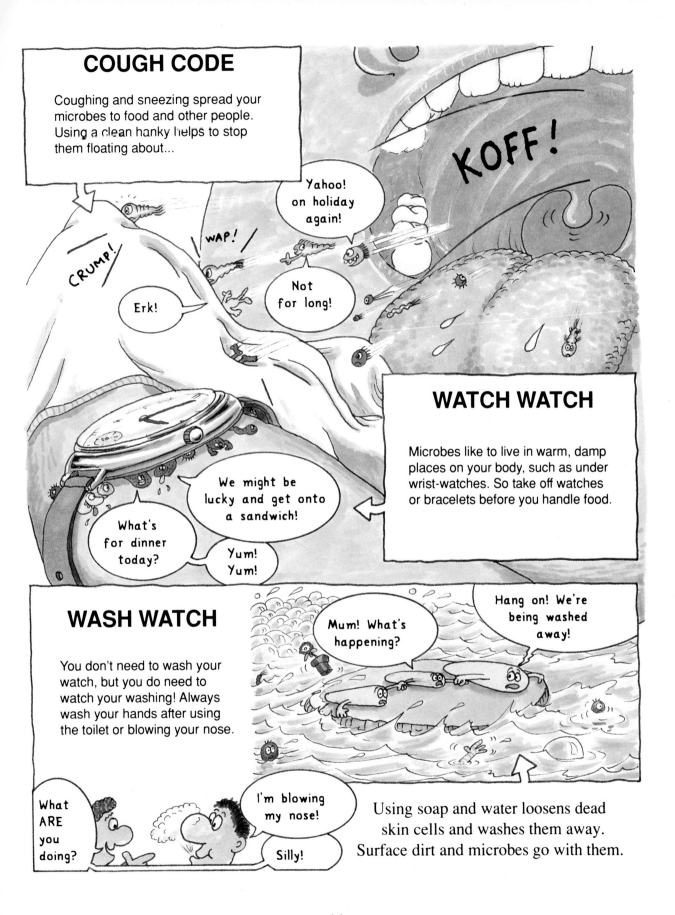

COUGH CODE

Coughing and sneezing spread your microbes to food and other people. Using a clean hanky helps to stop them floating about...

WATCH WATCH

Microbes like to live in warm, damp places on your body, such as under wrist-watches. So take off watches or bracelets before you handle food.

WASH WATCH

You don't need to wash your watch, but you do need to watch your washing! Always wash your hands after using the toilet or blowing your nose.

Using soap and water loosens dead skin cells and washes them away. Surface dirt and microbes go with them.

CATCHING GERMS...

FROM ANIMALS...

Illnesses aren't just carried by food. Sometimes microbes arrive from animals, especially in hot countries. For example...

Rabies from mammals

Malaria from mosquitos

Toxocariasis from dog-droppings

Bilharziasis from water-snails

Black Death from rat fleas

FROM PEOPLE...

Illnesses which spread from person to person are called infectious diseases. When a lot of people catch the same microbes over a short time, it's called an epidemic. It's easy to see how an epidemic can happen.

Let's play...

MICROBE TAG!..

Imagine you have a disease which can be spread by touching people.

All of the people you've touched today will touch lots of other people.

After a few days, there might be thousands of people with your disease.
That's why doctors tell you to stay at home when you're ill. And resting helps you to recover from most illnesses.

Eek!

Eek!

Eek!

Smallpox virus
magnified 150,000 times

HAVE YOU EVER HAD ANY

JABS??

You may not like having vaccinations – but they're better than having diseases! One disease you probably won't catch is SMALLPOX. This is a very infectious and often fatal disease.

In 1967 the World Health Organisation decided to get rid of it. It was a huge job. Doctors travelled the world looking for smallpox victims. They vaccinated everyone who might have caught the virus. By 1980, smallpox disease was wiped out!

Actually, there are a few samples of smallpox viruses locked up in research laboratories!

Let's hope they don't get out!

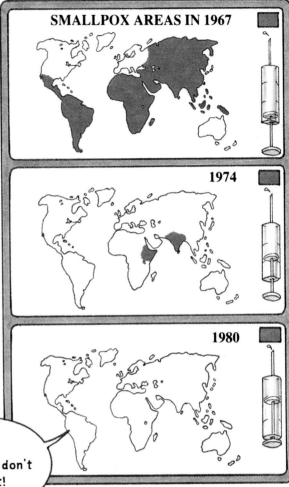

SMALLPOX AREAS IN 1967

1974

1980

Many more diseases could be controlled or cured. More food, hospitals and health education would save a lot of suffering.

BUT... these things cost a lot of money. Charities in rich countries help people in poor countries by giving them food, money and medicines.

CHARITY SPOT...

1. Look for charities in the phone book. Decide which ones you want to support.

2. Raise money for them at your school with Charity Days...

SEE NEXT PAGE

Here's a good idea for a School Charity Day event...

SPONSORED ILLNESSES!

1. Get your teacher to help you find out about microbe diseases.
2. Write and photocopy some leaflets describing different diseases and where they occur. Say how victims will be helped by a donation to charity.
3. Form yourselves into groups of two or three.
4. Choose the disease you're going to act out. Decide who is going to be the ill person. This person uses make-up to make them look ill.
5. The others can give out the leaflets and collect the money.

BLINDNESS

A few types of microbes cause blindness. Put on a blindfold and get someone to lead you round.

TYPHOID FEVER

A deadly disease caused by a Salmonella bacteria. Get some red powder paint and colour your skin with small blotches.

HERE ARE A FEW IDEAS!

DYSENTERY

Some bacteria and amoeba make people go to the toilet a lot. Young victims die of hunger and thirst. Stay in a toilet rattling your money tin.

YELLOW FEVER

Caused by a virus carried by mosquitoes. Paint your face yellow and pretend to be tired and ill.

Different microbes affect people in different ways. Doctors can often tell what a disease is by looking for particular signs of a disease. These signs are called symptoms. Most people can recognise flu symptoms...

FLU!

Influenza viruses magnified 200,000 times.

1. Flu viruses float about in the air...

Mmm! Fresh air!

SNIFF!

2. You breathe them in...

Close-up of cilia cells in your throat.

3. Some throat cells have tiny, waving hairs called cilia. They help to keep out dust and bacteria. The flu viruses invade the cilia cells and destroy them...

Sore throat!

4. Then bacteria and dust can get into your throat and lungs. Your throat feels sore and your chest hurts...

Flu!

CHOO!

5. You'll probably have a dry cough and a runny nose...

6. Your body gets hot. This affects your brain. You feel tired and have odd dreams...

YUK!

HACK!

WHEEZE!

7. After a few days, you feel better. Your cilia cells grow back. They waft the dust and bacteria up to your throat. You feel "chesty".

There are viruses everywhere, but you don't become ill every time you're infected. That's because your body has a wide variety of ways to fight off microbes!..

Your body's defences against microbes are called your

IMMUNE SYSTEM...

Inside your nose...

MUCUS

You swallow and breathe in billions of microbes every day. Many of them are dissolved and killed by chemicals in your saliva and nose mucus.

WHITE BLOOD CELLS

When microbes manage to get past your mucus, they're attacked by white blood cells. These patrol your body, searching for invaders. They gobble up things which don't belong in your body.

ANTIBODIES

When there are too many microbes for your white blood cells to catch, your body produces antibodies. These are chemicals which make microbes stick together. Then your white blood cells can catch them more easily. Antibodies may stay in your blood for years helping you to fight infections. Vaccinations help your body to produce antibodies which trap particular microbes.

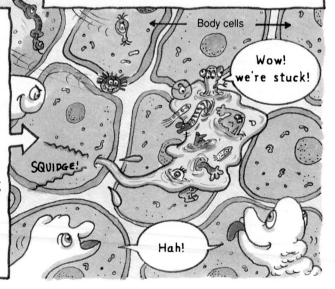

INTERFERON

Viruses can only grow inside living cells. Most of your white blood cells can't reach them there.

So your body cells produce a chemical called interferon which stops many viruses from growing.

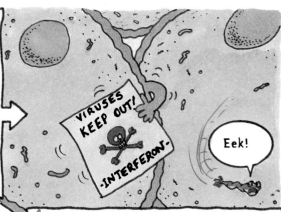

FEVER

When your other defences are struggling to cope, you get a temperature. Your raised body heat may kill some microbes and stop others from growing.

HAVE YOU BEEN INFECTED TODAY??

You're almost certain to have been infected by hundreds of different types of microbes!

You don't become ill each time – because your immune system protects you.

BUT... it needs to keep in practice. Regularly fighting off a few microbes keeps your immune system healthy and strong. Then if you're attacked by larger numbers, your body has a better chance of coping.

GERM-FREE ANIMALS FACT

Scientists in Japan have raised animals which are free of all microbes. These animals are weak and never grow properly.

And their immune system doesn't work. If they're infected by even a few ordinary microbes, they quickly die. They have to be protected from microbes at all times!..

17

It's hard to know what to do about germs. If you let too many in, you get ill. If you don't let enough in, your immune system becomes weak. Then you get ill! It's a bit of a...

GERM MAZE!

Pretend you're one of these microbes. You're trying to reach the people to infect them. Which microbe will get through the hygiene traps?

(NO SCRIBBLING!)

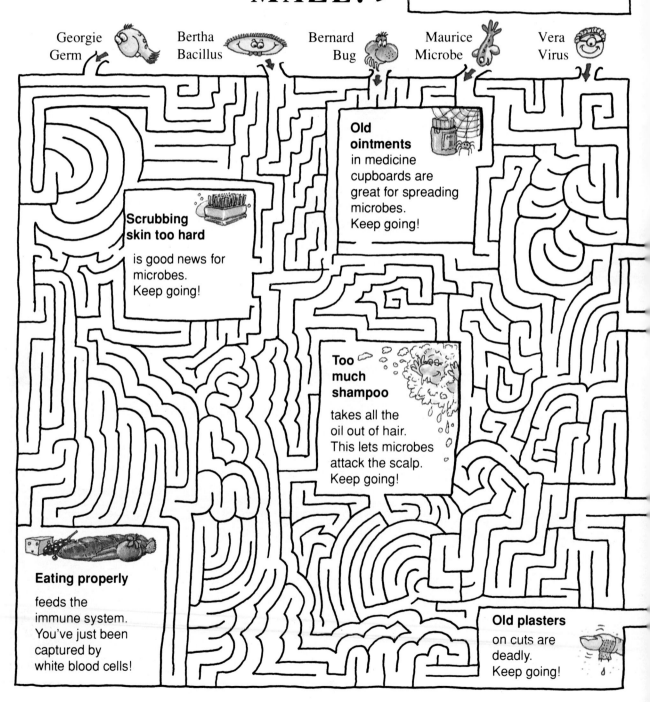

Georgie Germ

Bertha Bacillus

Bernard Bug

Maurice Microbe

Vera Virus

Old ointments in medicine cupboards are great for spreading microbes. Keep going!

Scrubbing skin too hard is good news for microbes. Keep going!

Too much shampoo takes all the oil out of hair. This lets microbes attack the scalp. Keep going!

Eating properly feeds the immune system. You've just been captured by white blood cells!

Old plasters on cuts are deadly. Keep going!

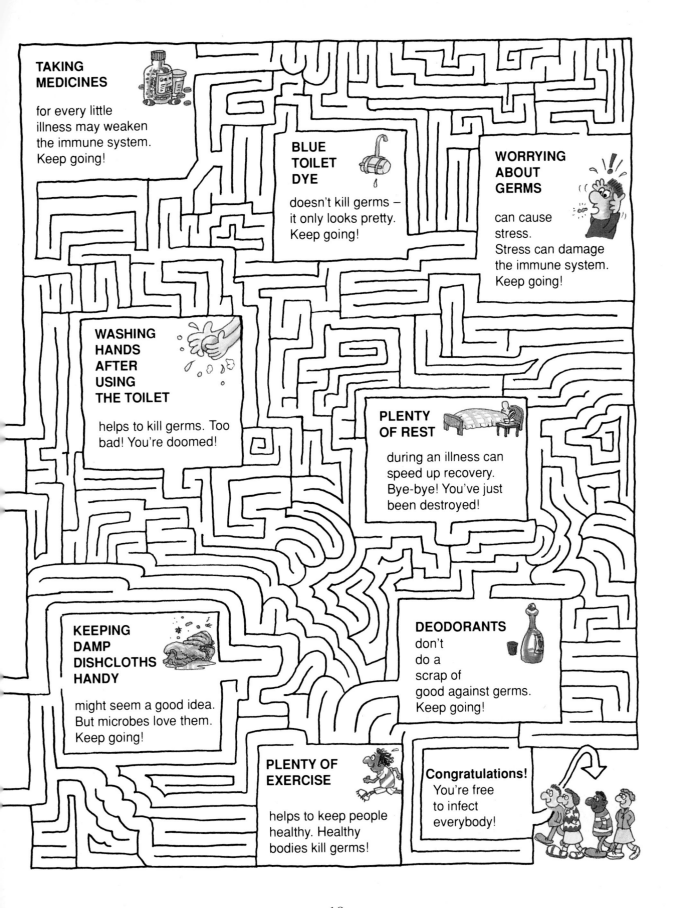

TAKING MEDICINES for every little illness may weaken the immune system. Keep going!

BLUE TOILET DYE doesn't kill germs — it only looks pretty. Keep going!

WORRYING ABOUT GERMS can cause stress. Stress can damage the immune system. Keep going!

WASHING HANDS AFTER USING THE TOILET helps to kill germs. Too bad! You're doomed!

PLENTY OF REST during an illness can speed up recovery. Bye-bye! You've just been destroyed!

KEEPING DAMP DISHCLOTHS HANDY might seem a good idea. But microbes love them. Keep going!

DEODORANTS don't do a scrap of good against germs. Keep going!

PLENTY OF EXERCISE helps to keep people healthy. Healthy bodies kill germs!

Congratulations! You're free to infect everybody!

GOOD VIRUSES

Microbes aren't all up to no good. Some viruses attack the bacteria which might attack you!
Right now, scientists are working on ways to cure ill people by using these viruses...

1. A virus research laboratory...

2. Viruses which attack bacteria are called Bacteriophages. One sort looks a bit like a lunar landing module!..

3. They're attracted by particular sorts of bacteria. They land on them...

4. They inject a chemical called viral DNA into the bacteria...

5. The DNA makes more of itself by hijacking the bacteria cell's energy and food supply...

6. New virus bodies form. The bacteria cell's food and energy are used up and it dies...

7. The new viruses burst out and land on other bacteria!

Dead bacteria

Microbes often have to fight each other for survival. Many use chemicals they produce as weapons. Doctors can use these chemical weapons as...

MICROBE MEDICINES!..

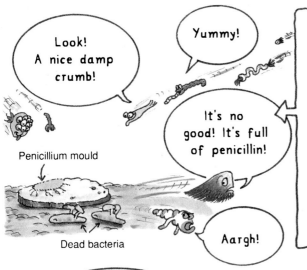

Look! A nice damp crumb!

Yummy!

It's no good! It's full of penicillin!

Aargh!

Penicillium mould

Dead bacteria

Some microbes make chemicals which kill off other microbes. These chemicals are called

ANTIBIOTICS.

The first antibiotic that doctors used as a medicine is called penicillin. It's made by a fungus which grows on bread. Doctors use lots of different antibiotics to destroy microbes.

And how are we today Mrs Wiggins? Still having funny dreams?

Yes doctor!

INSULIN

Insulin is a chemical produced by the body. It helps the body to use the sugar in food. People with a disease called diabetes don't produce enough insulin.
But scientists can now breed special types of bacteria which make insulin for us. Then it's injected into people with diabetes.

Do you remember interferon (page 17)?

INTERFERON

Interferon can also be made by bacteria. It can be injected into people whose immune system isn't working properly. Then they can fight off virus attacks more easily.

Microbes don't have mouths, but they can still take in food. Between them, they can "eat" just about anything. So their waste products can be almost anything too!

MICROBE MINERS...

People collect or dig up many different chemicals left behind by microbes. For example, bacteria helped to produce the valuable pure sulphur deposits which are mined in Mexico and Libya. This is how they did it...

This sulphur-making bacterium has a ridiculously long name for its size – Delsulphovibrio desulphuricans. Try saying that with your mouth full!

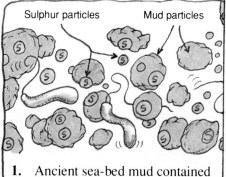

Sulphur particles   Mud particles

1. Ancient sea-bed mud contained sulphur mixed with other chemicals.

MUNCH!

MUNCH!

2. Bacteria which could eat the mud arrived.

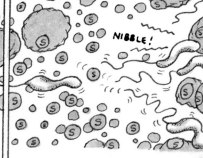

NIBBLE!

3. They ate the mud and left the sulphur behind.

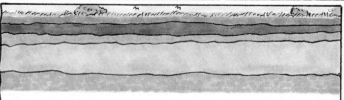

4. Thick layers of yellow sulphur built up. It became buried by rocks.

5. The sulphur is now dug up and used in industry.

"THAT TOOTHPASTE'S MINE!" FACT

Miners dig up ancient microbes too. Toothpaste makers use a fine white clay in their product. This clay is the bodies of billions of microbes which died millions of years ago!

My ancestors helped to make that!

Spoilsports!

Diatom

Tooth-decay bacteria

And what about plastic toothbrushes? Most plastic is made from oil. BUT...

WHERE DOES OIL COME FROM?

MICROBES MADE IT!

1. These are diatoms. They're tiny single algae cells. A litre of sea-water may be home for two billion diatoms!

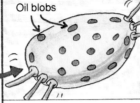

Oil blobs

2. Diatoms contain a sort of vegetable oil.

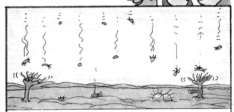

3. Diatoms lived in the sea millions of years ago too. When each died, its body fell to the sea-bed.

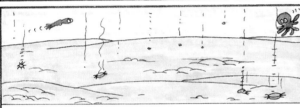

4. A muddy ooze of dead diatoms built up on the sea-bed.

5. More mud covered the diatoms. The oil squeezed out of their bodies. More mud fell.

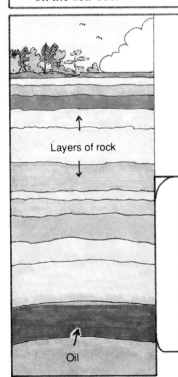

Layers of rock

Oil

6. After millions of years the diatom oil became buried under tons of rock.

7. In 1859, the world's first oil well was drilled in America. By 2059, all the underground oil will probably be used up!

Oil is called a fossil fuel because it's the remains of microbes which have been dead for millions of years. We're quickly using up our supplies of oil.
As well as for plastic and petrol, oil is also used to make fertilizers...

SEE NEXT PAGE

PLANTS EAT CHEMICALS!

All plants need water, light and food chemicals to grow and live. They use carbon dioxide and oxygen from the air. They get nitrogen and other chemicals from the soil. Plants use these chemicals to make more plant material.

Carbon dioxide, water and oxygen from the air.

Light and heat from the sun.

Potato plant

Soil chemicals from the soil.

Potatoes

GRO-KWIK

GRO-KWIK

Farm tractor spraying fertilizer

To provide cheap food, farmers need to grow lots of each crop. So they use fertilizers, which contain nitrogen, to help the crops to grow.

BUT... some farmers overdo it. Using too much artificial fertilizer can damage the soil. It becomes dry and dusty. If strong winds come along, all the soil may be blown away!

Wow! I'm being blown away!

WHOOSH!

Eek! Eek! Come back! Squeak!

This sometimes happens – because artificial fertilizers kill off some of the microbes which live in the soil. Soil microbes are vital for healthy soil...

MICROBES MAKE COWS MOO!

A cow's insides are a bit like a compost heap! Cows mostly eat grass and clover. But the trouble with these plants is that they're too tough for cows to digest. They need microbes to digest their food for them!..

Yummy!

Stomach

View inside a cow

A cow's four-part stomach is home for a thousand million million microbes. It's warm, airless, wet and full of food – just how they like it!

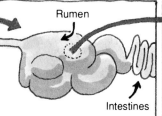

Rumen

Intestines

They live in the part of the stomach called the rumen.

Many of them are called cytophaga bacteria. They digest grass and turn it into food for the cow.

Munch! Munch!

Occasionally the cow brings up the grass from its rumen and re-chews it. This is called chewing the cud. Chewing the cud makes the grass particles smaller. This helps the microbes to digest them.

Thanks cow!

Thanks microbes!

When creatures live together and help each other like this, it's called symbiosis.

COW BELCH FACT

You may have heard cows mooing. Many people don't know that they're actually burping! Microbes in their stomach produce up to eighty litres of burp gas every day!

Moooo!

Oops – pardon me!

Granted!

All other grass-eating animals have microbes in their stomachs to help their digestion. So microbes help to make horses, sheep, rabbits and geese grow too!

Neigh!

Baa!

Nibble!

Honk!

Cows produce milk which is used to make yoghurt. And yoghurt is made by microbes too!

MAKE YOUR OWN YOGHURT!..

Why buy your yoghurt when I can make it for you at a quarter of the price??

Lactobacilli magnified 1200 times

1. Get a small tub of **live** yoghurt and a carton of UHT milk from a health-food shop.

2. Live yoghurt contains bacteria which have turned milk a tasty sort of sour!

3. Wash your hands, then put the milk in a clean bowl. Add a spoonful of the yoghurt. Cover the bowl with a clean plate.

Shoo!

4. Put it all in a warm place, keep it out of reach of cats!

About 25 degrees Centigrade

YOGHURT WATCH

5. Leave the bacteria to do its job for about twelve hours.

We must remember to save a spoonful for the next batch!

6. When the yoghurt sets, you can eat it. Add fruit to flavour it if you like.

AND... food and drink manufacturers use

MICROBE CHEFS

to help make all these products too!..

Cocoa   Tea   Coffee   Butter

Vinegar

Vitamin pills   Pickles   Cured ham   Tofu

Yeast extract   Chocolate   Monosodium glutamate for stock cubes   Soy sauce

Cider   Wine   Whisky   Beer   Bread

Cream   Buttermilk   Yoghurt   Koumiss   Cheese

Thanks microbes!

We rely on microbes for almost everything else we eat too. Microbes help make soil fertile so crops can be grown. And microbes help our farm animals to digest their plant food. In fact, without help from microbes, all animals would soon starve to death!

And bacteria are even used to make citric acid.

COMPLIMENTS OF THE CHEF

After you've eaten, you go to the toilet. An average person flushes away about fifty kilos of solid wastes a year. It all has to be dealt with somehow!

Fortunately...

MICROBES EAT EVERYTHING!

1. Sewage wastes contain dangerous bacteria and poisonous industrial chemicals. These can cause diseases when they're allowed to flow into rivers. So much of our waste is pumped to sewage treatment centres.

Microbes are used to make the sewage safe, or even useful!

There are thousands of types of microbes which help to make wastes safe. Here are just a few...

Volvox

Bacillus

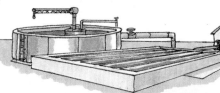

2. Wet sewage sludge is filtered through open tanks which contain microbes. This separates the liquids and the solids.

Micrococcus   Pseudomonas

Conidia

Euglypta

Thiotrix

The liquid is pumped into tanks containing microbes. Air is bubbled through.

The microbes purify the liquid.

Fine sludge goes back to the other tanks.

The water can be used again!

The solids go to heated underground tanks. Microbes digest the solids and turn them into safe, fine mud. This can be dried and used as fertilizer.

The microbes also give off methane gas. This gas is used to power and heat the treatment system!

Complicated isn't it? Never mind, we know what to do!

Actinophrys sol

Spirillum

Vorticella

As well as producing methane, and cow belch gas...

MICROBES MAKE AIR!

Microbes have been around since the very beginning of life on earth. That was about four billion years ago. The earth's atmosphere was very different at that time. It was made up of a mixture of gases which would be poisonous to humans.

The oxygen began to build up. After about three billion years, it made up about a fifth of the atmosphere – as it does today. Some microbes appeared which could use the oxygen. Then larger plants and animals appeared.

Ancient microbes lived in water and clay. They used chemicals for food and sunlight for energy. They gave off a waste gas called oxygen. This was poisonous for the microbes.

Most people wrongly think that trees produce most of the oxygen we breathe. Actually, almost all of the oxygen in the atmosphere is still produced by algae and bacteria!

Have you ever seen a TV advert for a disinfectant which "kills all known germs"?
Well – don't believe it!
Scientists have found several sorts of bacteria which **eat** disinfectants! And
anyway, you'd have to be barmy to want to kill off creatures which give you...

Medicines!

Clean water!

Food!

Air!

GERMS ARE GOOD FOR YOU!

They can live without us...

BUT WE CAN'T LIVE WITHOUT THEM!